D1414517

ISBN: 978-0-9909222-5-4

Unless otherwise noted, all Scripture quotes are taken from the HOLY BIBLE, NEW INTERNATIONAL VERSION˚. Copyright 1973, 1978, 1984 and 2011 by Biblica, Inc.˚ Used by permission. All rights reserved worldwide.

Printed in the United States of America

CONTENTS

TIPS FOR A
SUCCESSFUL STUDY

The study in your hands has the potential to change your life. So that you can get the most out of this experience, here are some recommendations and an overview about what to expect in each lesson.

This six-lesson study is designed to introduce you to what's going on in the criminal justice system—where we've gone right, and where we've gone wrong. In the context of a small-group community, you'll learn how you can engage with the criminal justice system, advocate for change, and make a difference. If you want to learn more and dig deeper into the topics, values, and Scripture that should guide our response to injustice, get a copy of our full-length book, also titled *Outrageous Justice*. While the book and the study stand alone, they also complement one another.

Over the next six lessons, you're going to learn a lot—if you're willing to engage. What you get out of this experience depends on what you're willing to put into it.

Before each session, read over the lesson to familiarize yourself with the Scriptures and even some of the questions. You don't need to do "homework" and write out your answers before the meeting, because part of what you'll be discussing will be presented via video when you gather. But knowing what to expect can give you some time to reflect and pray prior to the meeting. If you like, you can look up the Bible passages in another translation to compare them. (You can find about 40 different English translations on www.biblegateway.com or similar sites.)

Each session includes a video segment. The video begins with a welcome that offers a tip on having a successful group, followed by some real-life stories of people impacted by the criminal justice system, and wraps up with a brief teaching segment on that week's topic. The workbook will refer to what you learn in the video, but also to what you read. Before the meeting, be sure to have the video ready to play. Each lesson consists of the following components:

OPEN: These open-ended questions may feel light or simple, but they provide an opportunity for everyone to warm up to the discussion and get comfortable. Focus on listening carefully to other group members in order to get to know them better during this part of the meeting. Every person doesn't have to answer every

question. Let everyone share (or not) at the level that feels comfortable to them.

MEMORY VERSE: A memory verse is suggested at the beginning of each session that ties the topics back to the Bible. Encourage your group to commit these verses to memory.

LISTEN: Here, you will watch the video for the session. All of the videos are available at prisonfellowship.org/outrageousjustice/videos. If you prefer, you can request a DVD with all six sessions at prisonfellowship.org/outrageousjustice. Each session includes a short intro, followed by two people sharing the true stories of their lives, then a short teaching segment. Consider these storytellers as visitors to your group, who are telling of their experiences so you can respond to them.

READ: This section is a passage or two of Scripture. You'll have one person read it aloud, or you can ask several people to read, each reading just a few sentences.

RESPOND: This section allows you to learn by talking about the content you've read and watched and by listening to the insights of other group members. You'll go deeper in your dis-cussion of the teaching and storytelling, dig into Scripture, and wrestle with how to live out what you're learning. Again, there's no pressure. Share as much of your story as feels safe. And strive to make other group members feel comfortable by listening to them with empathy and compassion.

These are suggested steps you can take to dive deeper, learn more, or live out what you've learned. You can find a list of action steps associated with each session at prisonfellowship.org/outrageousjustice/action.

God cares deeply about justice and about every person. Through this study, you have the opportunity not just to learn about justice, but to expand your heart—love people, and care about justice, just as God does. Our hope is that God would meet you in the pages of this study and in the community of your small group.

JUSTICE THAT RESTORES
SESSION ONE

MEMORY VERSE

A bruised reed he will not break, and a smoldering wick he will not snuff out. In faithfulness he will bring forth justice; he will not falter or be discouraged till he establishes justice on earth. —Isaiah 42:3-4

A MOM HELD IN JAIL FOR A TRAFFIC TICKET.

A FATHER SENT TO PRISON FOR A DECADE FOR POSSESSING A SMALL AMOUNT OF MARIJUANA.

A YOUNG MAN SENTENCED TO LIFE IN PRISON FOR A CRIME HE DID NOT COMMIT.

EVERY DAY IN AMERICA, MORE THAN **30,000 PEOPLE** ARE ARRESTED. APPROXIMATELY **70 MILLION AMERICANS** HAVE A CRIMINAL RECORD OF SOME KIND.

Hearing these stories and stats, we might respond: "That's outrageous!"

It is outrageous. Our criminal justice system seems so huge, so complicated, and at times, riddled with injustice, that it makes us feel overwhelmed, angry, and outraged.

The Bible says God has an outrageous concern for justice, particularly for the poor and marginalized. He's outraged by injustice. But His forgiveness and goodness to us, even when we make huge mistakes or turn our backs on God, are also unexpected, amazing, and even outrageous.

Some people who are imprisoned, of course, have committed crimes and deserve to be punished. But increasing numbers of people in jail are there (or are at least there too long) because of flaws in the system: a lack of alternatives to incarceration, disproportional punishment, and even racial bias.

5

Justice is mentioned more than 130 times in the Bible, and it's at the core of God's character. God's justice is outrageous in the sense that it encompasses both just punishment as well as the opportunity for redemption. God wants each person to be treated fairly, with respect and dignity. When someone causes harm, justice may require punishment. Letting that person go unpunished would be unfair to the victim, to the community, to society at large, and even to the person who committed the crime. But God doesn't write people off. With love and kindness, He restores people and communities even through punishment, a process that human institutions can facilitate when they are based on restorative values—or obstruct when they are marred by injustice.

In this study, you're going to grapple with what justice is, how our system has gotten off track, and what you can do to bring back God's outrageous justice to our country.

CRIMINAL JUSTICE IN AMERICA

- **1 IN 115** AMERICANS INCARCERATED.

- **1 IN 28** K-12 STUDENTS HAS AN INCARCERATED PARENT.

- **1 IN 3** ADULTS HAS A CRIMINAL RECORD.

- MORE THAN **30,000** PEOPLE ARE BEING ARRESTED EACH DAY.

*AS OF 2017

OPEN YOUR GROUP

OPEN

■ Is there something you have seen in the news, or an incident that happened to you or a friend, that has made you second-guess justice in America?

_____

_____

_____

_____

_____

■ Tell about a time when you felt you were unfairly punished by a parent, teacher, or boss. What happened? How did that feel?

_____

_____

_____

_____

_____

Access the video for this session at
prisonfellowship.org/outrageousjustice/videos

SESSION NOTES

_____

_____

_____

_____

_____

_____

_____

_____

_____

_____

_____

_____

_____

_____

_____

_____

_____

_____

READ

But now apart from the law the righteousness of God has been made known, to which the Law and the Prophets testify. This righteousness is given through faith in Jesus Christ to all who believe. There is no difference between Jew and Gentile, for all have sinned and fall short of the glory of God, and all are justified freely by his grace through the redemption that came by Christ Jesus.

ROMANS 3:21-24

The Spirit of the Lord is on me, because he has anointed me to proclaim good news to the poor. He has sent me to proclaim freedom for the prisoners and recovery of sight for the blind, to set the oppressed free, to proclaim the year of the Lord's favor.

LUKE 4:18-19

RESPOND

■ In the video, you heard the story of Marlyn, a mom who ended up in jail because she didn't have $200 to pay a traffic ticket. How do you think a person's economic status affects their interactions with the justice system?

_____

_____

■ In the video, Craig said that even though we're created in the image of God and loved by God, we all fall short. The Romans 3 passage echoes this same truth. What does it mean to "fall short"? What are some ways that ordinary people often fall short?

_____

_____

■ In the video, Craig said, "What we call the problems in our culture are actually our solutions. …To take a violent act against another human being is to solve for the problem of fear, jealousy, or anger. To divorce our wife, to lie or get drunk, is the solution to the problems that are within us." In other words, we try to solve our problems by acting out. What we think is the "solution ultimately causes pain for ourselves and others." Tell about a time when you tried to solve a problem in a way that made things worse.

What does Romans 3:21-24 say about how we can attain righteousness? In other words, how can we satisfy God's justice and be made right with Him? (Romans 3:22)

_____

_____

■ What does it mean to be "justified freely by grace"? (Romans 3:24)

_____

_____

■ Through the prophet Isaiah, God told His people that He "loves justice" but "hates wrongdoing" (see Isaiah 61:8, quoted at the opening of this session). God offers grace but hates wrongdoing and crime. Is this inconsistent? How do these two ideas fit together?

_____

_____

■ In Luke 4, Jesus is reading aloud from the Old Testament prophet Isaiah, not only to define His mission, but to make it clear to His listeners that He was the Messiah. Looking at His words, what do you think He would say to the children of incarcerated parents? Or the parents of incarcerated young people?

_____

_____

■ What, if any, interaction have you had with people who are incarcerated or their families? (This might include your own family or yourself.)

_____

_____

■ Jesus mentions the poor, the prisoners, the blind, and the oppressed. What does Jesus say He will do for each of these groups? How do these groups overlap? As Jesus' followers, what are some practical ways we can continue His mission?

_____

_____

ANGEL TREE®
A Program of Prison Fellowship®

ANGEL TREE

For children with an incarcerated parent, experiences like summer camp may be out of reach. Thousands of children attend Christian camps each summer on an Angel Tree Camping® scholarship provided by Prison Fellowship.

ACTION STEPS

We are all at different places in our justice journey. Some of us are just starting out and need to learn more. Some of us know a lot but are trying to figure out how to put our knowledge into action.

What's one thing you want to do this week to grow in your understanding of the criminal justice system? You might want to research criminal justice issues or talk to someone you know who has been impacted by crime and incarceration, either directly or through a family member. You might even consider attending a criminal trial to see how the process works and how the defendant and victim are treated. You can also connect with Prison Fellowship on social media to stay informed and engaged. Links to our profiles can be found at prisonfellowship.org.

You can go to prisonfellowship.org/outrageousjustice/action for a more comprehensive list of action steps you can take individually or together as a group in response to this lesson.

To go deeper into the topics explored during this session, read chapters 1 through 3 in the *Outrageous Justice* book.

CLOSE BY PRAYING FOR YOUR GROUP

EXTRA NOTES

JUSTICE THAT RESPONDS
SESSION TWO

MEMORY VERSE

The Lord loves righteousness and justice;
the earth is full of his unfailing love.
—Psalm 33:5

Perhaps you've never been arrested—never had any dealings with the criminal justice system beyond a traffic ticket. Maybe you're lucky enough to have beaten the odds and have never been the victim of a crime.

You may be thinking, *The complex problems in the criminal justice system are unfortunate, but what do they have to do with me?*

In this lesson, we're going to talk about how to engage with the criminal justice system and why that is important. Every crime impacts three parties: the person who commits the crime, the victim or victims of that crime, and the community at large.

Even if you have never been arrested or been the victim of a crime, you're part of the community, so the justice system affects you. It is impossible to say, "it's not my problem," because crime and injustice affect the world we live in.

Beyond that self-interest, the Bible asks us to speak out for justice (see Proverbs 31:8-9). Jesus told us to visit prisoners. We have a duty and opportunity to engage.

The Bible tells us to follow the laws of the land and to do what is right. It also clearly calls us to not just avoid wrongdoing, but to advocate for justice, to speak up against injustice, and to visit prisoners. We are called to practice a justice that responds.

OPEN

■ What's one idea or concept from our last meeting that stuck with you during the week?

_____

_____

_____

_____

_____

_____

■ How do you think most people view those who are incarcerated? What assumptions do you think they make?

_____

_____

_____

_____

_____

_____

WATCH VIDEO

Access the video for this session at
prisonfellowship.org/outrageousjustice/videos

SESSION NOTES

_____

_____

_____

_____

_____

_____

_____

_____

_____

_____

_____

_____

_____

_____

_____

_____

_____

_____

_____

READ

Speak up for those who cannot speak for themselves, for the rights of all who are destitute. Speak up and judge fairly; defend the rights of the poor and needy.

PROVERBS 31:8-9 //

Then the King will say to those on his right, "Come, you who are blessed by my Father; take your inheritance, the kingdom prepared for you since the creation of the world. For I was hungry and you gave me something to eat, I was thirsty and you gave me something to drink, I was a stranger and you invited me in, I needed clothes and you clothed me, I was sick and you looked after me, I was in prison and you came to visit me."

Then the righteous will answer him, "Lord, when did we see you hungry and feed you, or thirsty and give you something to drink? When did we see you a stranger and invite you in, or needing clothes and clothe you? When did we see you sick or in prison and go to visit you?"

The King will reply, "Truly I tell you, whatever you did for one of the least of these brothers and sisters of mine, you did for me."

MATTHEW 25:34-40 //

RESPOND

■ Proverbs 31 says we should speak up for the poor and defend their rights. Do you think there is a correlation between being poor and being treated unjustly?

_____

_____

■ In the video, Craig DeRoche challenged us to care for the victims of crime and to advocate for just trials and just punishment. What do you think the Church's role (and your role) should be when it comes to criminal justice?

_____

_____

■ In Matthew 25, Jesus exhorts us to meet some basic human needs for under-resourced believers: food, shelter, clothing, health care. Why do you think visiting people in prison is included in this list?

_____

_____

■ What reward does Jesus promise to those who offer food, shelter, clothing, and visits to "the least of these"?

_____

_____

■ Have you ever visited a prison, jail, or juvenile detention facility? If so, briefly share your experience with the group. If not, what is your response to the idea of visiting people in prison?

_____

_____

■ What do you think Jesus meant when He said, "Truly I tell you, whatever you did for one of the least of these brothers and sisters of mine, you did for me"?

_____

_____

■ While some people are wrongfully accused and imprisoned, most prisoners are there because they committed a crime—they've sinned. Jesus, on the other hand, was sinless, the Son of God. In light of this contrast, why do you think Jesus said that when we visit prisoners we're visiting Him?

_____

_____

■ In the video, Craig invited us to "walk alongside the families of prisoners." What do you think that means? What is one way that you, as an individual or as a small group, could do that?

_____

_____

■ In the video, you heard from Quovodis Marshall, a former prisoner who is now a pastor. He described those who visited him in prison this way: "People who didn't know me, who should have seen me as their enemy, treated me like a friend." How can you be a friend to someone who is in prison?

_____

_____

■ In the video, Dan Trelka, police chief of Waterloo, Iowa, talked about how he and his wife have become foster parents, then adoptive parents, of children of prisoners. What is one way you could reach out to children impacted by the incarceration of one or both of their parents?

_____

_____

Angel Tree Camping gives children an opportunity to have fun, fellowship with their peers, build relationships with caring camp counselors, and experience the love of God in the great outdoors.

ANGEL TREE

ACTION STEPS

Do you know someone in your congregation or community that is currently incarcerated that you could write to or visit? If you don't know of someone currently incarcerated, consider requesting for your group to tour a local juvenile detention center, jail, or prison so you can see the correctional environment firsthand. Be respectful of the rules laid out by the correctional facility, but if possible, request to speak to the incarcerated youth, women, or men. Unless people proactively offer up their story, avoid asking how they got there. Seek to get to know them as you would anyone else. How do they spend their day? What do they enjoy doing? Do they have children or family nearby? It can mean a lot that you show concern and offer even a brief word of encouragement.

You can go to prisonfellowship.org/outrageousjustice/action for a more comprehensive list of action steps you can take individually or together as a group in response to this lesson.

To go deeper into the topics explored during this session, read chapters 4 and 9 in the *Outrageous Justice* book.

CLOSE BY PRAYING FOR YOUR GROUP

EXTRA NOTES

JUSTICE THAT LISTENS
SESSION THREE

MEMORY VERSE

Rejoice with those who rejoice;
mourn with those who mourn.
—Romans 12:15

OPEN

■ What's one idea or concept we discussed last week that you want to ask a question about?

_____

_____

_____

■ Tell about a time someone really listened to you. How did they do that? How did it make you feel when someone listened?

_____

_____

_____

_____

_____

_____

WATCH VIDEO

Access the video for this session at
prisonfellowship.org/outrageousjustice/videos

SESSION NOTES

_____

_____

_____

_____

_____

_____

_____

_____

_____

_____

_____

_____

_____

_____

_____

_____

_____

_____

_____

READ

On one occasion an expert in the law stood up to test Jesus. "Teacher," he asked, "what must I do to inherit eternal life?"

"What is written in the Law?" he replied. "How do you read it?"

He answered, "Love the Lord your God with all your heart and with all your soul and with all your strength and with all your mind"; and, "Love your neighbor as yourself."

"You have answered correctly," Jesus replied. "Do this and you will live."

But he wanted to justify himself, so he asked Jesus, "And who is my neighbor?"

In reply Jesus said: "A man was going down from Jerusalem to Jericho, when he was attacked by robbers. They stripped him of his clothes, beat him and went away, leaving him half dead. A priest happened to be going down the same road, and when he saw the man, he passed by on the other side. So too, a Levite, when he came to the place and saw him, passed by on the other side. But a Samaritan, as he traveled, came where the man was; and when he saw him, he took pity on him. He went to him and bandaged his wounds, pouring on oil and wine. Then he put the man on his own donkey, brought him to an inn and took care of him. The next day he took out two denarii and gave them to the innkeeper. 'Look after him,' he said, 'and when I return, I will reimburse you for any extra expense you may have.'

"Which of these three do you think was a neighbor to the man who fell into the hands of robbers?"

The expert in the law replied, "The one who had mercy on him."

Jesus told him, "Go and do likewise."

LUKE 10:25-37

RESPOND

■ In 2016, an estimated 15.9 million households in America experienced property crime, while 5.7 million people reported being victims of violent crimes. Have you ever been the victim of a crime? Briefly share what happened. What was your response to the situation? How did you feel?

_____

_____

■ In the video, Heather talked about validating victims' experiences. What do you think it means to validate someone? What are some things you could say or do to validate a victim's experience, or alternatively, what kind of comments or actions might invalidate their experience?

_____

_____

■ What does "mourning with those who mourn" have to do with our response to victims of crime?

_____

_____

■ Jesus tells the story of the Good Samaritan as a response to a question. What question is asked of Him? Who asks it? Why do you think Jesus responds with a story, followed by His own question, rather than answering directly?

_____

_____

Samaritans were the enemies of the Jews. The Jews, especially the religious leaders, hated Samaritans, in part because they believed Samaritans did not practice religion as they should. Why do you think Jesus chose to make a Samaritan the hero of the story?

_____

_____

In the story of the Good Samaritan, what did caring for the victim of crime cost the Samaritan? Look at the text and make a mental note of the things he provided. On a scale of 1 to 10, how generous was the Samaritan?

_____

_____

What does this parable tell us about God's heart toward victims of crime? What does it tell us about how to live out our faith? What mandate does it provide for Christians?

_____

_____

In the video, you heard from Alison, whose home was set on fire by an arsonist. The arsonist rationalized the crime by saying "no one was hurt," but Alison pointed out that her family was indeed very hurt and traumatized by the crime. What did you learn about how to respond to victims of crime from her story?

_____

_____

RESPOND (continued)

■ In the video, you heard Bethany's story about a burglary. She said, "I don't want to live my life out of a sense of fear, constantly trying to plan ahead to block the possibility of discomfort." Why do you think Bethany and her roommates choose to live where they do? She also said that God does not call us to be "safe." Do you agree or disagree with her statement?

_____

_____

■ What is one way you can reach out to a victim of crime in your community and provide practical help to them? How can your church community assist and support victims of crime?

_____

_____

■ In the video, Heather talked about the difference between forgiveness and reconciliation. How would you explain this difference? Can you think of a time when reconciliation between a victim and the person who harmed them would not be appropriate or helpful?

_____

_____

ANGEL TREE

A Program of Prison Fellowship®

ANGEL TREE

Children of prisoners are sometimes called the invisible victims of crime. Prison Fellowship's Angel Tree Sports Clinic™ provides an opportunity for these boys and girls to be seen, validated, and mentored by caring adults during an unforgettable event.

ACTION STEPS

Do you know of someone recently harmed by crime in your congregation or community? Do they have practical needs you could offer to meet, like attending trials as a source of support, making repairs, replacing what was taken, or spending time just sitting and listening?

No matter how much time has passed since the crime, don't forget to keep asking how the victim is doing and if there is anything you can do. The journey to restoration can be a long one.

Please visit prisonfellowship.org/outrageousjustice/action for a more comprehensive list of action steps you can take individually or collectively in response to this lesson and associated resources.

To go deeper into the topics explored during this session, read chapter 6 in the *Outrageous Justice* book.

CLOSE BY PRAYING FOR YOUR GROUP

EXTRA NOTES

JUSTICE THAT FITS
SESSION FOUR

MEMORY VERSE

Do not pervert justice; do not show partiality to the poor or favoritism to the great, but judge your neighbor fairly.

—Leviticus 19:15

The punishment, most people believe, should fit the crime. In fact, fair and appropriate punishment is part of the very definition of justice. There's a lot more to consider when we talk about justice, of course: the care of victims, fair treatment of those accused of crime, opportunities for rehabilitation, and so on. But justice should ensure that crime is punished with a fitting penalty, whether it is a fine, incarceration, community service, or monetary restitution.

There is something within us that cries "foul" when someone gets off with a sentence that's too lenient. And we feel the same sense of outrage when someone is given a punishment that's too harsh. Neither extreme is just.

Unfortunately, for the last several decades, the United States has erred on the side of harsh punishments. In an effort to "get tough on crime," courts have often handed down disproportional sentences. The result: staggering fines for seemingly minor infractions, countless cases where the punishment does not fit the crime, and excessively long sentences that keep women, men, and young people from contributing to their families and communities.

Should crime be punished? Absolutely. To let it go unpunished would be as unjust as punishing too harshly. But we must grapple with the difficult question of what is appropriate, proportional punishment.

In this lesson, you're going to learn about some ways that the criminal justice system has gotten off track, and what you can do to help bring about change. God cares about justice and fairness, and is outraged by disproportional punishment.

We, too, should be outraged by it and be willing to advocate for justice and speak out for those who cannot speak for themselves.

CRIMINAL JUSTICE IN AMERICA

- **MORE THAN 10.5 MILLION ARRESTS WERE MADE IN AMERICA IN 2016.** THE HIGHEST NUMBER OF THESE ARRESTS WAS FOR DRUG ABUSE VIOLATIONS (1,572,579), FOLLOWED BY LARCENY OR THEFT (1,050,058), AND DRIVING UNDER THE INFLUENCE (1,017,808).

- **ONLY 3 PERCENT OF AMERICANS CHARGED** WITH A FEDERAL CRIME WILL RECEIVE A JURY TRIAL.

- **LESS THAN 5 PERCENT OF AMERICANS CHARGED** WITH A STATE CRIME WILL RECEIVE A JURY TRIAL.

- **AS OF 2013, 1 IN EVERY 6 FORMAL CASES IN JUVENILE COURT WAS ON THE BASIS OF STATUS OFFENSES.** OF THESE, 55 PERCENT WERE ON THE BASIS OF TRUANCY CHARGES (CHARGING A YOUNG PERSON CRIMINALLY FOR FAILURE TO ATTEND COMPULSORY PUBLIC SCHOOLING).

OPEN YOUR GROUP

OPEN

◼ What has surprised you most about this group?

_____

_____

_____

◼ Tell about a time you received what seemed to be a disproportional
punishment—perhaps as a child. How did you respond? What was that
experience like for you?

_____

_____

_____

_____

_____

Access the video for this session at
prisonfellowship.org/outrageousjustice/videos

SESSION NOTES

_____

_____

_____

_____

_____

_____

_____

_____

_____

_____

_____

_____

_____

_____

_____

_____

_____

_____

_____

READ

If people quarrel and one person hits another with a stone or with their fist and the victim does not die but is confined to bed, the one who struck the blow will not be held liable if the other can get up and walk around outside with a staff; however, the guilty party must pay the injured person for any loss of time and see that the victim is completely healed....

But if there is serious injury, you are to take life for life, eye for eye, tooth for tooth, hand for hand, foot for foot, burn for burn, wound for wound, bruise for bruise. An owner who hits a male or female slave in the eye and destroys it must let the slave go free to compensate for the eye.

And an owner who knocks out the tooth of a male or female slave must let the slave go free to compensate for the tooth.

EXODUS 21:18-19, 23-27

Do not spread false reports. Do not help a guilty person by being a malicious witness.

Do not follow the crowd in doing wrong. When you give testimony in a lawsuit, do not pervert justice by siding with the crowd, and do not show favoritism to a poor person in a lawsuit.

If you come across your enemy's ox or donkey wandering off, be sure to return it. If you see the donkey of someone who hates you fallen down under its load, do not leave it there; be sure you help them with it.

Do not deny justice to your poor people in their lawsuits. Have nothing to do with a false charge and do not put an innocent or honest person to death, for I will not acquit the guilty.

Do not accept a bribe, for a bribe blinds those who see and twists the words of the innocent.

Do not oppress a foreigner; you yourselves know how it feels to be foreigners, because you were foreigners in Egypt.

EXODUS 23:1-9

RESPOND

▥ In the opening question, you shared stories of times you personally received disproportional punishment. How did that experience impact your ability to empathize with those who are unfairly punished?

_____

_____

▥ Look at the verses from Exodus 21. Why do you think God spelled out crimes and punishments so specifically? What does the passage say was proportional punishment for someone who injured a slave?

_____

_____

▥ In the video, Heather said, "Just as it's an injustice to ignore oppression, it's also an injustice to punish someone beyond what they deserve." What do you think drove the trend toward harsher sentencing or continues to make it difficult to reform sentencing today?

_____

_____

▥ In the video, Heather talked about the problem of over-criminalization. There are so many laws about so many different things that people could break a law without intending to, or even realizing that what they did is against the law. Have you ever broken the law without realizing or intending to? How do you think our country got so many laws? What good intentions might have motivated lawmakers and those they represent?

_____

_____

■ In the video, Debi shared her story about being incarcerated for 16 years for a nonviolent crime, although there was no physical evidence, and she had no criminal record. Do you feel that her punishment was fair and in just proportion to her crime? What did she and her family lose as a result of her punishment?

_____

_____

■ How might having a mother in jail instead of with her family cause damage to the community at large? (In other words, how might Debi's problem become society's problem?)

_____

_____

■ The passage from Exodus 23 tells us not to "pervert justice." What does it mean to "pervert justice"? In what ways has justice been perverted in our culture?

_____

_____

■ Exodus 23 also warns us to not deny justice to the poor. Why would God have to warn us about that? How does a lack of resources impact a person's ability to receive justice?

_____

_____

■ Do you think that people who lack resources are treated differently than the wealthy or even the middle class in the U.S. justice system? What about people of different races? Why or why not?

_____

_____

■ What do you think the Church's role ought to be in promoting sentencing that fits? What are some practical ways that your church or even your small group could get involved?

_____

_____

ACTION STEPS

Here's something everyone can do this week:
Go to prisonfellowship.org/advocacyalerts and sign up to join Prison
Fellowship's Justice Advocate network. As a Justice Advocate, you will have
access to digital campaigns that help you identify your elected officials and
quickly contact them using model social media posts, emails, and call scripts
that we provide.

If you want to take your advocacy to the next level, consider applying to be a
Justice Ambassador. Justice Ambassadors are the select Justice Advocates in
our network who are equipped by Prison Fellowship to:

- Develop relationships with lawmakers through calls, letters, and in-person
  meetings to encourage support for justice reforms.
- Write letters to the editor in your local paper reflecting Prison Fellowship's
  views on justice issues.
- Host awareness-building events on campus, at church, or in your
  community.

You can learn more and apply to be a Justice Ambassador at
prisonfellowship.org/justiceambassador and discover additional action steps
at prisonfellowship.org/outrageousjustice/action.

To go deeper into the topics explored during this session, read chapter 5 in the
Outrageous Justice book.

CLOSE BY PRAYING FOR YOUR GROUP

EXTRA NOTES

JUSTICE THAT TRANSFORMS
SESSION FIVE

MEMORY VERSE

May the groans of the prisoners come before you;
with your strong arm preserve those condemned to die.
—Psalm 79:11

The word "culture" can describe customs, arts, and social institutions of a group of people, as well as the attitudes and behaviors characteristic of a particular social group.

We can talk about the culture of a country or locale, or of certain groups of people (such as "the drug culture"), or even the culture of a business or institution.

Have you ever worked at a company, or perhaps attended a school, where the culture was positive and supportive? Businesses and colleges pay attention to building a constructive culture because it typically improves their bottom line and helps them attract high-quality people.

For many, the phrase "prison culture" might evoke images of violence, despair, or fear. So what would it look like to have a constructive prison culture? That may seem like an oxymoron. But it's possible. A constructive prison culture emphasizes the positive. It is safe, structured, and supportive. A constructive culture invites, even facilitates, transformation.

Jails and prisons don't have to be warehouses for human beings. They can be places that facilitate rehabilitation by providing opportunities to make amends and earn back the public's trust. They can be places that enable people to leave as productive members of society, rather than just teaching them how to "improve" their criminal behavior.

As Christians, we can advocate for constructive culture in our prisons. Transformation is rarely easy, but it is always worthwhile.

ANGEL TREE

OPEN

■ What's one thing from last week's discussion (on over-criminalization and proportional punishment) that stuck with you since we last met?

_____

_____

_____

_____

■ What do you think of when you hear the term "constructive culture"? For example, what would a constructive culture look like in a school?

_____

_____

_____

■ What would a constructive culture look like in a corporation or family?

_____

_____

_____

WATCH VIDEO

Access the video for this session at
prisonfellowship.org/outrageousjustice/videos

SESSION NOTES

_____

_____

_____

_____

_____

_____

_____

_____

_____

_____

_____

_____

_____

_____

_____

_____

_____

_____

_____

_____

_____

_____

_____

_____

_____

_____

_____

_____

_____

_____

_____

_____

_____

_____

_____

_____

_____

_____

_____

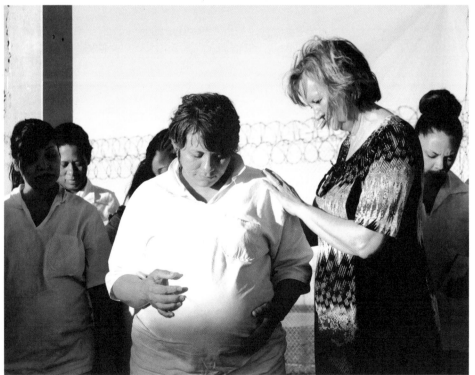

READ

The crowd joined in the attack against Paul and Silas, and the magistrates ordered them to be stripped and beaten with rods. After they had been severely flogged, they were thrown into prison, and the jailer was commanded to guard them carefully. When he received these orders, he put them in the inner cell and fastened their feet in the stocks.

About midnight Paul and Silas were praying and singing hymns to God, and the other prisoners were listening to them. Suddenly there was such a violent earthquake that the foundations of the prison were shaken. At once all the prison doors flew open, and everyone's chains came loose. The jailer woke up, and when he saw the prison doors open, he drew his sword and was about to kill himself because he thought the prisoners had escaped. But Paul shouted, "Don't harm yourself! We are all here!"

ACTS 16:22-28

Continue to remember those in prison as if you were together with them in prison, and those who are mistreated as if you yourselves were suffering.

HEBREWS 13:3

RESPOND

■ Tell about a time in your life when you found yourself in a negative culture—perhaps in school, at work, or even in a church? Describe what that was like. What factors contributed to the culture? How did it impact the people in that environment? How did it impact you?

_____

_____

■ In your opinion, are people who are incarcerated likely to change for the better while in prison? Explain.

_____

_____

■ In Acts 16, Paul and Silas are falsely accused, then severely beaten and imprisoned. Were they treated justly? What would you have done if you'd experienced what they did?

_____

_____

■ What were Paul and Silas doing while stuck in prison? What does that tell you about them?

_____

_____

■ Why didn't Paul and Silas run away from the prison when the earthquake occurred? How did they change the culture of the prison they were in?

_____

_____

In the video, Jesse talked about countering the current cultural values in our prisons, like suspicion, violence, and deceit, and instead, promoting the values of trust, peace, and honesty. What is your response to this idea?

_____

_____

How would a toxic prison culture lead to higher rates of recidivism (people who commit new crimes and return to prison)?

_____

_____

Hebrews 13 echoes Jesus' command to visit those in prison. How would visiting prisoners impact the culture in a prison? What impact would you expect to see from visiting someone in prison for a single event or worship service compared to long-term discipleship of an incarcerated man or woman, lasting even after release from prison?

_____

_____

In the video, Jesse challenged us to "walk alongside families, offering emotional and practical support." What, if anything, stirred in you when you heard that? How could you walk alongside a family of someone who is incarcerated?

_____

_____

In the video, you heard from Randy Grounds, a former warden in a maximum-security prison. What steps did he take to change the culture in that prison?

_____

_____

You also heard from Nick Robbins, who was formerly incarcerated. How did Nick change from the time he entered prison until he was released? What caused that transformation? What surprised you about his story?

_____

_____

SECOND CHANCE 5K

Every April, Prison Fellowship and its partners celebrate a nationwide Second Chance™ Month to raise awareness of the collateral consequences of a criminal conviction and unlock second-chance opportunities for people who have paid their debt to society.

ACTION STEPS

The video named several ways people on the outside can impact prison culture: visiting (and discipling) prisoners, supporting wardens and staff, and providing support for families of prisoners. Prison Fellowship offers training and programs across the country to do just that. Even if there isn't a prison near where you live, Prison Fellowship's Angel Tree program, which provides Christmas gifts to children on behalf of their incarcerated parent, is a great way to get involved. Visit prisonfellowship.org/outrageousjustice/action for a menu of action steps that you can take in response to this lesson.

To go deeper into the topics explored during this session, read chapter 7 in the *Outrageous Justice* book.

CLOSE BY PRAYING FOR YOUR GROUP

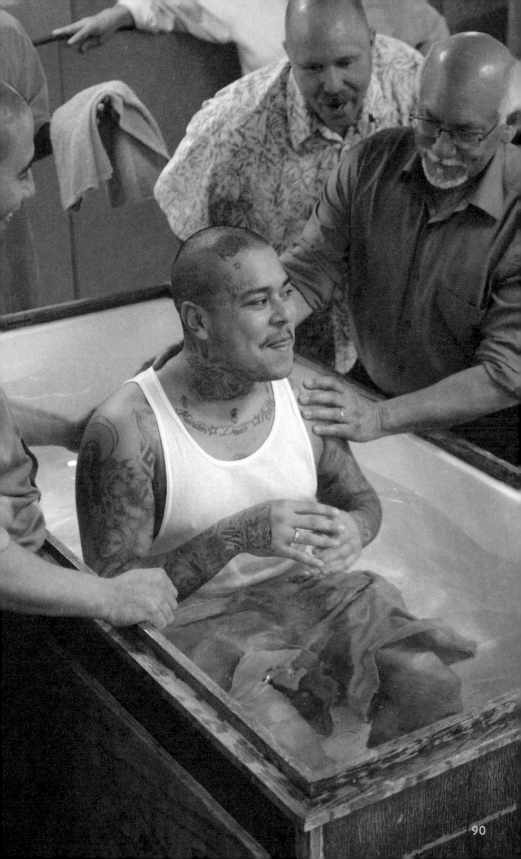

EXTRA NOTES

JUSTICE THAT REDEEMS
SESSION SIX

MEMORY VERSE

So from now on we regard no one from a worldly point of view.
...Therefore, if anyone is in Christ, the new creation has come:
The old has gone, the new is here!
—2 Corinthians 5:16-17

OPEN

■ What has surprised you most about this group?

_____

_____

_____

■ What have you enjoyed most about this group?

_____

_____

_____

■ What does it mean to get a second chance after you've done something wrong? Tell about a time you got a second chance.

_____

_____

_____

SECOND CHANCE MONTH

Every person has dignity and potential. But 1 in 3 American adults has a criminal record, which limits their access to education, jobs, housing, and more. They are living in a "second prison" that keeps them from reaching their full, God-given potential. Since launching the first Second Chance Month in 2017, Prison Fellowship has spearheaded the nationwide effort to raise awareness about these barriers and unlock brighter futures for people with a criminal record. Together, we can open the door for approximately 70 million Americans to live up to their potential after paying their debt to society!

VISIT **PRISONFELLOWSHIP.ORG/SECONDCHANCES** TO LEARN MORE.

WATCH VIDEO

Access the video for this session at
prisonfellowship.org/outrageousjustice/videos

SESSION NOTES

READ

So from now on we regard no one from a worldly point of view. Though we once regarded Christ in this way, we do so no longer. Therefore, if anyone is in Christ, the new creation has come: The old has gone, the new is here! All this is from God, who reconciled us to himself through Christ and gave us the ministry of reconciliation: that God was reconciling the world to himself in Christ, not counting people's sins against them. And he has committed to us the message of reconciliation.

2 CORINTHIANS 5:16-18

Perhaps the reason [Onesimus] was separated from you for a little while was that you might have him back forever—no longer as a slave, but better than a slave, as a dear brother. He is very dear to me but even dearer to you, both as a fellow man and as a brother in the Lord.

PHILEMON 1:15-16

ROAD TO SECOND CHANCES PRAYER WALK

RESPOND

- In the video, Jesse described the lifelong restrictions placed on people with a criminal record as a "second prison." How might these restrictions make it difficult for formerly incarcerated people to become productive members of society?

_____

_____

- What does it mean to "pay your debt to society" by serving time in prison? Is that debt ever completely paid? Explain.

_____

_____

- The passage from 2 Corinthians defines reconciliation as "not counting people's sins against them" and says we've been given a ministry of reconciliation. How can we carry out that ministry when it comes to people with criminal histories?

_____

_____

- In the video, you heard from Gina. What obstacles did she face as she tried to reintegrate into society after serving her prison sentence? What surprised you about her story?

_____

_____

- In the passage from Philemon, what is Paul asking Philemon to do? In light of the culture at that time, which Jesse talked about in the video, what do you think Philemon's response was to this request?

_____

_____

In the video, Jesse said, "Business owners can be part of unlocking second chances for people trapped in the second prison by hiring people with a criminal history." What benefits to a business or a community might there be to this business strategy?

_____

_____

What happens to a person when we describe them as a "criminal" or "felon" or "convict"? How does our view of them, and perhaps their view of themselves, change when we use words like "person with a criminal history"? How does that subtle change help us to follow Paul's recommendation in Philemon (whom Paul said had been a slave, but was now a brother)?

_____

_____

If you were to welcome someone returning home from prison as a brother or sister in the Lord, what sort of things would you do? How would you treat them? What would you say?

_____

_____

As you reflect on the things you've learned and the way God has met you in this study, perhaps you have a sense that you want to share it with others. Pray and listen. Is God inviting you to take this study and lead it with another group of people? Even if you've never led a group, God might be asking you to step out in faith and try it.

_____

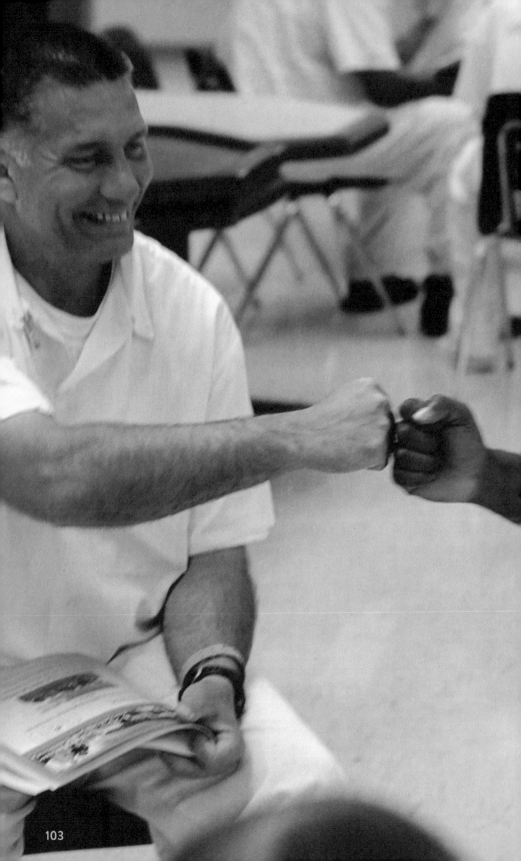

104

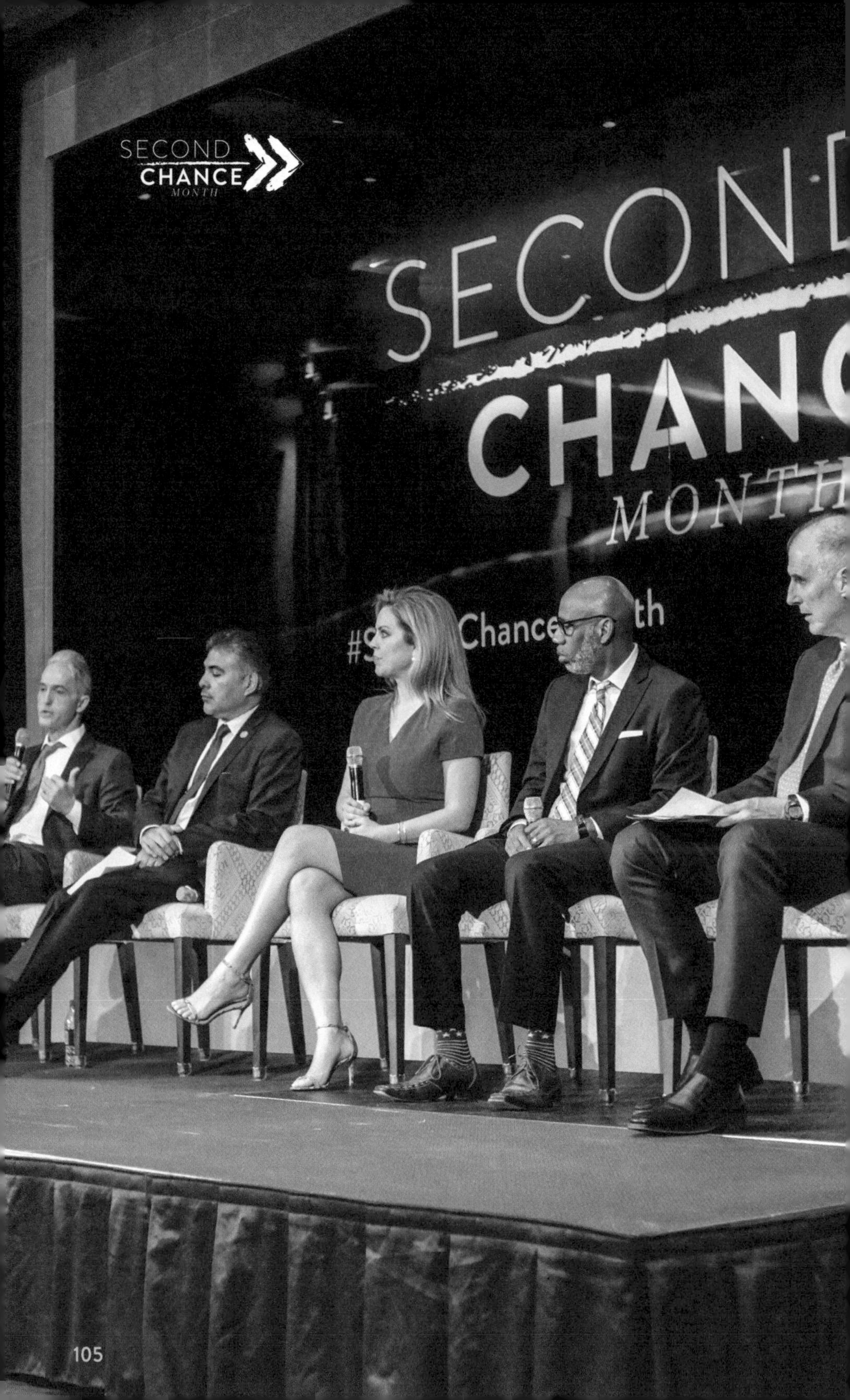
SECOND
CHANCE
MONTH

ACTION STEPS

As discussed in the lesson, one of the easiest things we can do is to change the way we talk. We are firm believers that language can change culture over time. Instead of using terms like "offender," "felon," "convict," or even "ex-offender," try using terms that affirm each person's God-given dignity first and foremost. You may be surprised at how much saying "person with criminal history" instead of "ex-con" communicates about the potential you see in them to those who have been through the criminal justice system.

You can go to prisonfellowship.org/outrageousjustice/action for a more comprehensive list of action steps related to meeting reentry needs in your community and participating in Second Chance Month.

To go deeper into the topics explored during this session, read chapter 8 in the *Outrageous Justice* book.

CLOSE BY PRAYING FOR YOUR GROUP

EXTRA NOTES

Prison Fellowship® was founded in 1976 by Charles Colson, a former aide to President Nixon who spent seven months in prison for a Watergate-related crime. Today, it is the nation's largest Christian nonprofit serving prisoners, former prisoners, and their families, and a leading advocate for criminal justice reform. Through an amazing awakening to new hope and life purpose, those who once broke the law are transformed and mobilized to serve their neighbors, replacing the cycle of crime with a cycle of renewal.

Prison Fellowship staff and volunteers are in hundreds of correctional facilities each day, sharing the Gospel, spreading hope, and teaching life-changing classes. Through our evangelism events, we introduce incarcerated men and women to a new future in Christ and nurture their spiritual growth with Bible studies and intensive discipleship courses. We also offer a holistic set of classes and intensive programs to prepare prisoners to be leaders in their communities—whether inside or outside of prison. As a result, we are seeing prisoners use their sentences as a time to grow, change, and find a new, positive life path with Prison Fellowship staff and volunteers as their guides.

You can go to prisonfellowship.org/outrageousjustice/action for a more comprehensive list of action steps to help you put what you've learned in this group into practice.